A LOOK AT LIFE IN

The Eighties

Adrian Gilbert

First published in 1999 by
Wayland Publishers Ltd,
61 Western Road,
Hove,
East Sussex BN3 1JD

This book was prepared for Wayland Publishers Ltd
by Ruth Nason.

Series editor: Alex Woolf
Series design: Stonecastle Graphics/Carole Design
Book design: Ruth Nason

Find Wayland on the internet at:
http://www.wayland.co.uk

British Library Cataloguing in Publication Data

Gilbert, Adrian
A look at life in the eighties
1. History, Modern - 20th century - Juvenile
literature
2. Nineteen eighties - Juvenile literature
I. Title II. Eighties
909.8'28

ISBN 0 7502 2469 X

Printed and bound in Italy by G. Canale & C.S.p.A.,
Turin

Cover photographs

Top left: Mikhail Gorbachev and Ronald
Reagan in Red Square, Moscow, May
1988 (Topham Picturepoint)

Top right: Arnold Schwarzenegger in
The Terminator (Orion, courtesy Kobal)

Centre: The space shuttle *Discovery*
heads for Earth orbit, September 1988
(Popperfoto)

Bottom left: The Louvre pyramid, Paris
(Topham Picturepoint)

Bottom right: Madonna, 1987 (Topham
Picturepoint)

Acknowledgements

The Author and Publishers thank the following
for their permission to reproduce photographs:
Camera Press: pages 4b, 5b, 6, 7t, 7b, 10b, 11t, 11b,
12b, 14-15b, 16t, 18b, 19, 20t, 22t, 22b, 23b, 25t,
26, 27t, 27b, 28-29t, 29b, 30b, 31t, 31b, 34b, 37b,
39, 40t, 40b; Robert Harding Picture Library: pages
12t, 14t, 18t; Popperfoto: pages 8, 9t, 9b, 10t, 17,
25b, 32, 33t, 33b, 34t, 35t, 35b; Retna Pictures:
pages 21, 23t, 24; Science Photo Library: pages
4-5t (Alex Bartel), 13 (Phillip Hayson), 15t (Joyce
Photographics); Spelling/ABC (courtesy Kobal):
page 36b; Topham Picturepoint: pages 16b, 28b,
30t, 36-37t; Touchstone/Amblin (courtesy Kobal):
page 38b; Universal (courtesy Kobal): page 38t.

Contents

A Look at...

...in the '80s

A LOOK AT
THE NEWS
IN THE '80s

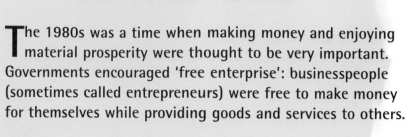

▷ New technology enabled stock exchanges around the world to share information instantly.

The 1980s was a time when making money and enjoying material prosperity were thought to be very important. Governments encouraged 'free enterprise': businesspeople (sometimes called entrepreneurs) were free to make money for themselves while providing goods and services to others.

Reagan and Thatcher

Ronald Reagan became president of the USA in 1981. As well as encouraging free enterprise, he tried to reduce the amount of money spent by the government, so that people would need to pay fewer taxes.

Margaret Thatcher explained, half-jokingly, how she ran her government:

'I don't mind how much my ministers talk, as long as they do what I say.'

As US president, Reagan found a friend and ally in the British prime minister, Margaret Thatcher. She was a very strong-minded person, admired by some people but bitterly disliked by others. Like Reagan, she wanted to reduce the role that government played in people's lives. Both leaders believed that individuals should be free to make their own decisions about jobs and money, rather than being told what to do by the government.

Money markets

The financial world was very important in the 1980s. Many of the old laws which had

▽ President Reagan (left) and Margaret Thatcher were among the representatives to a United Nations conference held in Cancun, Mexico, in 1981. (See page 46 for a list of everyone in the picture.)

controlled stock markets and banks were removed, in what became known as 'deregulation'. At the same time, new computerized electronic trading systems were introduced, which enabled stockbrokers to buy and sell shares without delay. These developments led to an international financial system, where enterprising individuals could make (and lose) fortunes within minutes, just by trading shares.

▷ *During the 1980s many people became homeless and were forced to live on city streets.*

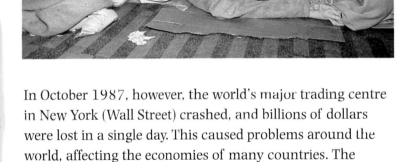

...Newsflash...

Washington DC, 30 March 1981. President Ronald Reagan was shot in the chest today as he walked to his car. Two of his aides were also wounded when John W. Hinckley fired a hail of shots. Reagan was rushed to the George Washington University Hospital where he underwent two hours of surgery. His doctors expect him to make a full recovery. He quipped to his wife Nancy: 'Honey, I forgot to duck.' The motives for the assassination attempt are unknown. Hinckley will undergo psychiatric testing before facing trial.

In October 1987, however, the world's major trading centre in New York (Wall Street) crashed, and billions of dollars were lost in a single day. This caused problems around the world, affecting the economies of many countries. The 1987 crash was the start of a recession, which meant that unemployment increased and people had less to spend.

Many of the unemployed came from the old manufacturing and mining industries like coal, steel and shipbuilding. It was very hard for them to find new jobs, and this caused great distress, not only to the unemployed and their families but to the whole communities in which they lived.

Cold War warriors
Reagan and Thatcher were both strongly opposed to communism, and during the 1980s they encouraged opposition to communist regimes, especially the Soviet Union. The USA increased the size of its armed forces and began the SDI (Strategic Defence Initiative) or 'Star Wars'

programme. The idea was to build rockets and lasers capable of shooting down Soviet missiles while they were still in space. Although the SDI was eventually abandoned, it was an example of how the Cold War (the rivalry between communist states and those of the Western world) got worse in the 1980s.

At the end of 1979, the Soviet Union had invaded Afghanistan to prevent the communist Afghan government from being taken over by local Islamic rebels. Many Western governments decided to support the rebels.

△ Afghan rebels, known as 'mujahidin' (holy warriors).

...Newsflash...

Grenada, 6 November 1983.
The tiny Caribbean island of Grenada has come under American control. US troops invaded the island on 31 October, to get rid of the new communist government of Bernard Coard. Although supported by Cuban military advisers, Coard's forces were unable to repel the attack. President Reagan says that he needed to protect the 1,000 Americans living in Grenada, but it is probable that he wishes to give other nations in Central America the message that he will not tolerate extreme left-wing regimes so close to the USA.

They sent arms and equipment to aid the rebels in their fight against the Soviet army. The war lasted until the Soviets withdrew in 1988, but fighting in Afghanistan between rival rebel groups continued well into the 1990s.

In Central America and the Caribbean, the USA aided groups or governments fighting against socialists and communists. The USA gave arms and money to the 'Contras', who fought the socialist but democratically elected government of Nicaragua. In the neighbouring country of El Salvador, the USA financed the right-wing government in its war against left-wing (socialist) rebels.

Global wars
There were many wars, fought all round the world, during the 1980s. Argentina invaded the Falkland Islands in 1982. Though close to Argentina, the islands were a British territory and the people living there wanted to stay British. After the Argentinian invasion, Britain sent a naval Task Force to the Falklands. During fighting between the air forces and the navies of Britain and Argentina, a small British army was landed on the islands. After several pitched battles, the Argentinians were forced to surrender and return the Falklands to British control.

Also in 1982, Israel's army entered Lebanon, a country from which Palestinian terrorists of the PLO (Palestine Liberation Organization) made attacks on Israel. The Palestinians fought the invading Israelis, and both sides suffered heavy casualties. Eventually, the better-armed Israelis forced the PLO out of Lebanon, but many towns and cities were destroyed, including much of the Lebanese capital of Beirut.

▷ *Muslim women in Lebanon march behind a portrait of Ayatollah Khomeini, who ruled in Iran.*

▽ *Fighting in Lebanon left the capital, Beirut, severely damaged.*

Islamic fundamentalism

The Israeli invasion of the predominantly Arab state of Lebanon caused great anger throughout the Islamic world. The 1980s was a time when many people of the Islamic faith became increasingly angry at what they saw as the injustices suffered by their people. This anger was combined with the growth of Islamic fundamentalism, a movement which believed in the strict observance of the Islamic faith.

Hardline fundamentalist groups used violence to promote their aims, and even attacked the governments of their own countries if they thought they were not religious enough. But, above all, Islamic fundamentalists were opposed to the state of Israel and those nations in the West who supported Israel.

After the overthrow of the Shah (or king) in 1979, Iran was governed by extremist Islamic religious leaders under the overall rule of Ayatollah Khomeini. Iran now became a centre for extreme anti-Western views. Although Iran was engaged in a brutal war with its neighbour Iraq, it still found time and resources to support terrorists fighting Israel and the West.

...Newsflash...

Sakhalin Island, 15 September 1983. Soviet sources have admitted that a Korean 747 jet liner, Flight 007, which disappeared off the Soviet island of Sakhalin on 1 September, was shot down by one of their fighter aircraft. All 269 passengers, including 61 Americans, were killed. The incident has caused uproar in the USA and the Senate has condemned the action as a 'brutal massacre'. It is a mystery why the aircraft was shot down. The Soviets claim that Flight 007 was flying through restricted air space without navigation lights, and imply it was being used for spying purposes.

Hijacking and hostage-taking

The hijacking or destruction of passenger aircraft had become a common form of terrorism during the 1970s, and this continued into the 1980s. In 1985, an Iranian-backed Lebanese group hijacked a TWA plane flying from Athens to Rome. The group took 39 hostages to a hide-out in Beirut, and later managed to exchange them for 735 Islamic fundamentalists held in Israeli prisons.

Not all attacks on aircraft were made by Islamic groups, however. A Korean 747 jet liner was shot down by Soviet fighters in 1983, killing 269 passengers.

The pilot of the hijacked TWA flight radioed to his flight controllers:

'They are beating up the passengers. We must land in Beirut. He has pulled a hand-grenade pin and is ready to blow up the aircraft ...'

Another type of terrorism was the kidnapping of foreigners working in the Lebanon. During the 1980s, 23 people – Americans, Indians, Saudi Arabians and Europeans – were taken hostage by the Iranian-backed Hezbollah (Party of God). The hostages were held in very bad conditions and were harshly treated by their captors. Several of them died in captivity. But towards the end of the decade the survivors slowly began to be released.

◁ *Terry Waite (left), adviser to the Archbishop of Canterbury, went to Lebanon to negotiate the release of hostages, and fourteen were freed in 1982-86, as a result of his work. He was taken hostage himself in 1987, and freed only in 1991.*

Profile

Cory Aquino (1933 -)

The wife of a Philippines politician, Corazon (Cory) Aquino entered politics when her husband was assassinated in 1983. They both opposed the corrupt dictator Ferdinand Marcos. In 1986, after a rigged election, pressure from the ordinary people of the Philippines forced Marcos to flee the country, and Cory Aquino was appointed president. She faced many problems as the new leader, but she brought real democracy to her country. In 1992 she decided not to enter the new elections and retired from politics.

Democratic progress

Although most people who lived in Europe and the USA enjoyed democratic government, having a real say in how their lives were run, other people around the world were not so lucky. But some progress towards democracy was made in the 1980s. The people of the Philippines overthrew the corrupt government of Ferdinand Marcos in 1986. The leader of the peaceful revolution, Cory Aquino, freed political prisoners and restored democratic institutions, such as free speech and regular elections.

In Spain, the democratic government faced a great challenge in 1981, when a gang of right-wing army officers took over the Spanish parliament by force, in a plot to overthrow the government. The rest of the army backed the government, however, and King Juan Carlos went on television to denounce the plotters. Supported by the Spanish people, the army units loyal to the government surrounded the plotters, who were then forced to surrender.

▽ Army officers storm into the Spanish parliament, Madrid, 2 February 1981.

▷ *Tiananmen Square, Peking, June 1989: defying the tanks sent in to end demonstrations for reform.*

Other advances for democracy took place in South America, where free elections were held in Chile, Argentina and Brazil, countries which had previously been under the control of the armed forces. In China, however, the democratic movement failed in 1989, when tanks of the Chinese army crushed a revolt by students in Peking's Tiananmen Square.

The troubles continue

In Northern Ireland, Catholic republican groups attempted to get rid of the British presence, and the situation continued to be violent. Hunger strikes by republican prisoners were followed by assassinations and bombings. The only ray of hope in this confrontation came in 1985, when the governments of Britain and the Irish Republic made an agreement to work together on Northern Irish affairs.

The end of communism

The most important news story of the decade was the ending of the Cold War and the collapse of communism. In 1980, Polish trade unionists formed the 'Solidarity' group to

Profile — Mikhail Gorbachev (1931 -)

When he became leader of the Soviet Union in 1985, Mikhail Gorbachev began to reform the communist system. He developed the policies of Glasnost (openness) and Perestroika (rebuilding) and he tried to make the economy more efficient. Gorbachev called for friendship between the communist countries and the West, and he played a leading role in getting both sides to reduce nuclear weapons. But towards the end of the 1980s, growing economic problems within the Soviet Union made him less popular with the ordinary people.

▷ *In Poland, Lech Walesa (right) led the out-lawed Solidarity movement throughout the '80s. In 1989 he was elected president of the country.*

oppose their communist government, but they had limited success. The real change was made by Mikhail Gorbachev, who came to power in the Soviet Union in 1985. He worked hard to improve relations with the West, he withdrew Soviet troops from Afghanistan, and he reduced the numbers of Soviet nuclear weapons. His reforms in the Soviet Union encouraged people in communist-dominated Eastern Europe to get rid of their rulers.

The end of communism in Eastern Europe happened incredibly quickly in the second half of 1989. In June, proper elections were held in Poland and the communists were replaced by the new Solidarity party. On 10 November, the Berlin Wall, which divided communist East Berlin from West Berlin, was torn down. This was the first stage of the reunification of East and Western Germany.

▽ *East German soldiers break through the Berlin Wall, 1989.*

> **❝ ❞**
>
> West Germany's chancellor, Helmut Kohl, welcomed the destruction of the Berlin Wall by the people of East Germany:
>
> **'We're on your side; we are and remain one nation. We belong together.'**

On 21 November, the Czech Communist Party accepted opposition demands to hold multi-party elections. Democratic reforms were announced in both Bulgaria and Yugoslavia on 15 December, and on 17 December the overthrow of the communist regime began in Romania.

A LOOK AT
SCIENCE and TECHNOLOGY
IN THE '80s

The speed of change in the world of science and technology seemed to get faster than ever. There were advances in the field of computers and electronics, and in space travel. But the environment continued to be a problem and, despite the best efforts of many scientists, there were major disasters that caused widespread pollution.

The first ever PCs (Personal Computers) had been invented in the 1970s, but they were expensive and too complex for anyone but a computer expert to use. The great breakthrough in PC development came in 1981, when the US manufacturer IBM (International Business Machines) introduced its own PC.

The key to the importance of the IBM PC lay in its software. It used a new operating system developed by the US Microsoft Corporation in

△ Electric typewriters were put aside, in favour of PCs, which could be used for word processing.

1977, called MS-DOS (Microsoft Disc Operating System), which was much easier to use than the older systems. The IBM PC also used the

Profile

Bill Gates (1955 -)

One of the first people to understand that computers would become a major part of everybody's life was Bill Gates. He made a fortune by developing software programs with his Microsoft Corporation, a company he set up in Seattle, in 1977. His big break came in the early 1980s, when IBM introduced its Personal Computer (PC). IBM gave a licence to Microsoft to develop software that would enable non-computer specialists to use the new PCs. Soon a Microsoft operating system was being used in virtually every computer sold around the world.

latest, highly advanced silicon chips developed by the Intel Corporation, which enabled the computers to be small yet powerful. The IBM PC helped transform the computer world because it allowed ordinary people to use computers for the first time.

Computers worldwide

The new IBM PC proved a great success. In 1981, 25,000 machines were sold; just three years later the figure had soared to three million. During the 1980s, other computer manufacturers began to develop similar machines – called 'clones' – and soon PCs were being used worldwide. At first their main use was in the office, but by the end of the decade PCs were being used in the home too. They proved very popular with children, who used them for educational purposes and to play computer games.

Bruce Sterling wrote in 1986:

'Eighties tech sticks to the skin, responds to the touch: the personal computer, the portable telephone, the soft contact lens.'

The miniaturization of computer components was not used only in PCs. Microcomputers were employed in all sorts of modern machines, such as cars, washing machines, telephones – even toasters!

Goodbye
Telexes;
mechanical
wristwatches

Hello
Compact discs;
CD-ROMs;
personal stereos;
mobile phones;
camcorders;
TV satellite dishes

A revolution in communications

The 1980s computer explosion was part of a greater revolution in the communication of information. Telephone systems provided new opportunities to transmit data. Although fax (short for 'facsimile') machines had been introduced in the 1970s, it was not until 1980 that they became an effective means of communication by using ordinary telephone lines. By the mid-1980s even the smallest companies had a fax machine as part of their basic office equipment. And soon fax machines were used in many homes, allowing people to send each other documents at the press of a button.

Another 1980s development using telephone lines to communicate information was the modem. This simple device linked computers to each other, so they could relay messages and documents. The modem was the first step towards the linking up of computers into the World Wide Web and the Internet.

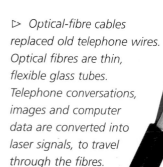

▷ Optical-fibre cables replaced old telephone wires. Optical fibres are thin, flexible glass tubes. Telephone conversations, images and computer data are converted into laser signals, to travel through the fibres.

Environmental issues

Although scientists and people working in the field of technology made many great advances, they were unable to solve the old problems of pollution. Efforts were made to make industry more 'clean and green', but environmental problems remained serious.

Acid rain became an international political issue in 1982, when Canada accused the USA of causing environmental damage. Acid rain is produced when gases in exhaust fumes from burning fuel react with water in the air to form acids. When the rain falls, it causes harm to plants and animals. The Canadians said that acid rain had drifted northwards from the industrial areas of the USA and had fallen on Canadian lakes and rivers, killing large numbers of fish.

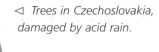

◁ *Trees in Czechoslovakia, damaged by acid rain.*

Acid rain was also a major problem in Europe during the 1970s and 1980s, especially in parts of West Germany and Scandinavia. The European nations acted quickly to reduce emissions of the most harmful gases, making acid rain less damaging. But the USA was slow to do anything to solve this problem.

New political parties giving top priority to environmental issues gained support in the 1980s. David Icke, spokesman for the Green Party in the UK, said:

'Green politics is not about being far left or far right, but about being far-sighted.'

A hole in the sky

In 1985 scientists confirmed the existence of a 'hole' in the ozone layer of the earth's atmosphere. The ozone layer normally reflects harmful ultra-violet rays from the sun. A hole in it allows this radiation to reach the earth. The scientists explained that the hole in the air, high above the South Pole in Antarctica, had been caused by man-made chemicals called CFCs, which were used in aerosol spray cans, refrigerators and air-conditioning units.

It was found that CFCs also contributed to the 'greenhouse effect' which was causing the world slowly to get hotter (also

...Newsflash...

Auckland, New Zealand, 23 July 1985. More information has been revealed about the mysterious sinking of the Greenpeace ship *Rainbow Warrior* on 10 July 1985. The French secret service was behind the explosion which sank the ship at its moorings in Auckland harbour, killing a freelance photographer. The ship had been used by the environmental organization Greenpeace to protest at France's nuclear testing on remote Pacific islands.

▷ *A researcher in Antarctica launches a weather balloon to obtain information about the upper atmosphere.*

called global warming). In response to scientists' warnings about the dangers, 53 industrial countries signed the Montreal Accords in 1987 – an agreement to stop using CFCs by 2000.

Global disasters

An accidental leak of poisonous gases from the Bhopal chemical plant in India, on 3 December 1984, killed 2,000 people almost immediately and left 200,000 sick or injured. It was the worst ever industrial disaster. The plant made pesticides, designed to kill insects eating crops, but the disaster showed that technology could be dangerous, hurting the very people it was trying to help.

In April 1986, a major disaster occurred at a nuclear power plant near the Ukrainian city of Chernobyl in the Soviet Union. A full-scale nuclear melt-down took place, and fires burned for two weeks, allowing radioactive material to escape into the atmosphere.

◁ *Scientists check radiation levels in fields around Chernobyl, 1986.*

What made the Chernobyl disaster so serious was that radioactive material was carried around the world in the atmosphere. Many crops in Europe were affected and had to be destroyed and, in Scandinavia, milk was found to have 15 times the normal radiation level.

The melt-down occurred because of the reactor's poor design and a lack of proper safety measures. People around the world now began to worry that their own nuclear reactors might not be as safe as they had thought.

▽ A space shuttle is launched, 1983. Sometimes shuttles carry scientific experiments. Sometimes they carry satellites to launch into space, or take the astronauts to satellites which need repairing.

▷ Three of Saturn's moons, discovered by Voyager 2, can be seen on the left of this picture.

Final frontiers

Space exploration captured the public's imagination during the 1980s. The USA's two unmanned Voyager probes began to send back superb pictures of the planets in our solar system. Although launched in 1977, it was not until August 1981 that Voyager 2 reached Saturn, where it discovered eight 'moons' that had been too small to see from Earth.

The USA launched its first space shuttle, called *Columbia*, in 1981. The space shuttle was the first re-usable spacecraft. It was launched like a rocket, but it flew like an aircraft; once it had completed a mission it glided back through the atmosphere to Earth. The *Columbia* mission was a success, but the launch of the *Challenger* shuttle in 1986 ended in tragedy. Despite this setback, the USA continued to use space shuttles to send men and women into space.

Medical advances and setbacks

The world's first mechanical heart was successfully used in 1982 as a means of keeping a patient alive for a long period until a donor heart was found. Keyhole surgery – a new way of operating on people – also became popular. The surgeon needed to make only a small cut into the patient's body, and then, using miniaturized surgical instruments, performed the operation looking through a camera lens inside the patient's body.

In 1980 the World Health Organization announced that the killer disease smallpox had been eradicated. Smallpox had been one of the world's most deadly diseases – as recently as 1967 two million people had been killed by smallpox every year.

Unfortunately, the success of the medical profession in getting rid of smallpox was countered a year later by the announcement, on 5 June 1981, of the existence of a new disease called AIDS (Acquired Immune Deficiency Syndrome). Although scientists were not sure how the disease originated, it was transmitted through blood and other bodily fluids. AIDS was a killer disease and it soon spread throughout the world, with a number of African countries being particularly hard hit. By the early 1990s, an estimated three million people had contracted AIDS.

People who had AIDS were often shunned. As one AIDS sufferer explained:

'I have a terrible feeling that I am dying not from the virus, but from being untouchable.'

▽ *Adverts like this one from Australia gave the message that people must protect themselves against AIDS.*

AIDS.
PREVENTION IS THE ONLY CURE WE'VE GOT

...Newsflash...

Cape Canaveral, Florida, 28 January 1986. After 73 seconds of what seemed a routine launch, the space shuttle *Challenger* suddenly exploded in mid-air. Watched by millions of stunned people across the globe, the explosion killed all seven crew members instantly. Among them was Christa McAuliffe, a school teacher from New Hampshire, who had won a nationwide competition to fly in the shuttle. A set of faulty gaskets joining rocket-booster sections have been blamed for the disaster.

A LOOK AT FASHION IN THE '80s

The 1980s was a decade when people liked to show off their wealth, and one way of doing so was to wear expensive clothes. One of the most significant fashion trends of the first half of the 1980s was 'power dressing'. Clothes worn by 'power dressers' – who included both men and women – were very smart and were intended to impress people with the money and power of the wearer.

▷ Shoulder pads were 'in', especially in women's business clothes, as part of power dressing.

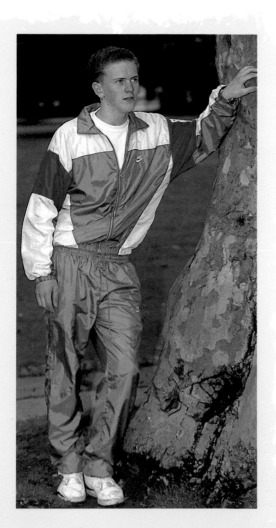

◁ Shell suits became very popular for children and adults.

This was the decade of the 'Yuppie' – a name made up from the words Young Upwardly Mobile Professional. Most Yuppies worked in the financial centres of major cities, like New York, London and Frankfurt, and they loved to wear expensive clothes. After the great financial crash of 1987 and the recession that followed, Yuppies faded from the scene.

Designer labels

Clothes made by top fashion designers became increasingly important to very large numbers of people. Previously, these clothes were worn only by a few select individuals, such as pop stars and TV celebrities. But, in the 1980s, ordinary people were prepared to pay to own clothes with the label of a famous designer. Many designers and manufacturers made fortunes by supplying the public's taste for clothes with fashionable designer labels.

Goodbye
Flared trousers;
tank tops;
permed hair
for men

Hello
Shoulder pads (for
men and women);
stonewashed jeans;
shell suits;
trainers

Established fashion names, such as Ralph Lauren and Calvin Klein, were joined by those of new designers, who included Bruce Oldfield, Issey Miyake and Jasper Conran. Many of the clothes they designed for the catwalk were deliberately outrageous, and this ensured that they received a great deal of attention from the fashion press.

▷ *Among the 1980s ideas of British designer Vivienne Westwood were the mini crinoline and underwear worn as outerwear. Designer Jean Paul Gaultier took up the underwear as outerwear idea, and Madonna made it famous.*

Top Japanese fashion designer Issey Miyake said this about his clothes:

'Without the wearer's ingenuity, my clothing isn't clothing. These are clothes where room is left for wearers to make things their own.'

...Newsflash...

Paris, June 1981. The famous Paris fashion show has been taken by storm by the new collection from a Japanese design group called 'Comme des Garçons'. This new wave of Japanese designers, who include Issey Miyake, Rei Kawakubo and Yohji Yammamoto, have thrown down a challenge to Western fashion ideas. The designers refuse to use bright colours. Their collection features loose-fitting clothes produced from new materials used in exciting and unusual ways.

International fashion
The old fashion centres of Paris and Milan began to face competition from designers in Japan, Britain and the USA. In many cases, these young designers made reputations on their own first, and then moved to the major fashion houses to carry on their careers. Inside the older fashion houses, there were a number of top designers who kept them in touch with modern fashion. They included Karl Lagerfeld at Chanel and Erik Mortensen at Pierre Balmain.

The Italian Georgio Armani established his reputation as a designer of high-quality clothes for men and women. It was said that he made women's clothes more masculine and men's clothes more feminine! One of Armani's greatest strengths was his skill in marketing his clothes to people of all types around the world. To own Armani clothes became an important international status symbol.

▷ *Armani-designed clothes modelled in Milan in 1989.*

Girls ahead

Just as fashion designers became household names, so too did the models who wore their clothes. This was the beginning of the age of the supermodel, women who were paid fortunes to wear top designer clothes. Among the new breed of supermodel were Jerry Hall and Christie Brinkley. Their faces were seen on the covers of magazines around the world. In the 1990s they would become as famous as film stars.

◁ *Model Christie Brinkley, with singer Billy Joel, whose hit song 'Uptown Girl' was about Christie.*

Triumph of the trainer

Another, very different trend began to emerge in the 1980s. This was based on people's interest in sport and other leisure activities. Track suits, once used only by athletes and other sports people, now began to be worn by adults and children for everyday wear. Women carried this idea further by wearing joggers and leggings outside the gym. But the single most important item of this new fashion was the trainer. The trainer originated from the simple canvas shoe and rubber plimsoll, but by the 1980s it had become a hi-

Athlete Jackie Aiyepong explained
the attraction of trainers:

**'They're the only thing the
whole world can relate to.
Actors, musicians, politicians,
everybody has got a pair
of trainers.'**

People's enthusiasm for designer labels
extended to the new sports-leisure world as
well, so that, for example, parents had to buy
their children the 'right' trainer or track suit.

Advertising

Manufacturers – and companies and
organizations that had nothing to do with
clothes – began to realize that they could
make money by putting their names on fashion
goods. People were prepared to pay extra for
clothes and other items bearing the name of
a company with an image that was considered
'cool'. And when people walked around in
these clothes, they gave the company some
free advertising too! The companies that were
considered 'cool' tended to be those operating
in sports and leisure, which appealed to young
people. Major football teams, for example,

tech piece of running equipment, utilizing the
latest materials. Companies specializing in this
footwear – such as Nike and Adidas – fought
each other desperately to persuade people to
buy their products.
During the decade,
sales of trainers
soared, and in the
USA average
ownership of
trainers doubled.

started to sell
products displaying
their name, such as
jackets, trousers,
backpacks and even
duvets.

This was part of
an overall trend
called licensed
merchandising – the
manufacture and sale
of a range of goods,
including pens, toys
and jewellery, as well
as clothes, to go with
a film, for example,
or anything that was
fashionable at the
time.

▷ At a concert in
Philadelphia in 1986,
rap artists Run DMC
invited the audience to
wave their trainers in
the air while the group
performed: 'We
make a mean team
my Adidas and me.'

A LOOK AT
POP MUSIC
IN THE '80s

▽ *Paul Simon (left) with South African musicians Miriam Makeba and Hugh Masekela.*

Popular music in the 1980s combined lots of different influences from around the world. The great explosion of Punk and New Wave that had shaken music in the late 1970s had begun to die down. Many old Punk groups, such as the Sex Pistols, disbanded, while others became part of mainstream pop.

A noticeable trend in pop in the early 1980s was the emergence of the New Romantics, who wore colourful clothes and did not take their music too seriously. They included Culture Club, Adam and the Ants, Duran Duran and Spandau Ballet. Other new groups, such as Wham!, also sang about the fun side of life.

World music

A more serious type of music to emerge was world music, a combination of international musical styles. In practice, this meant using folk music from Africa, Asia or South America and combining it with Western pop rhythms and instruments.

In 1982, rock musician Peter Gabriel organized the first WOMAD (World of Music, Arts and

Profile

Madonna (1958 –)

Her full name was Madonna Louise Ciccone, and she moved from Rochester, Minnesota, to New York to seek her fortune in the music business. Her first single 'Everybody' became a 1982 hit in the dance clubs, and was followed by a string of hits which made her a star around the world. Madonna was very good at judging the mood of the pop world, and she changed her image to fit whatever was happening at the moment. By the end of the decade she was the owner of her own film, publishing and recording companies.

▷ *The Irish group U2 made a great impact with their albums 'The Unforgettable Fire' (1985) and 'The Joshua Tree' (1987).*

Dance) festival, which brought together musicians from around the world. From then on, WOMAD became a focus for world music.

Many other Western musicians began to look around the world for inspiration. Among these was the US rock star Paul Simon, who went to South Africa to work with local musicians. The result was the famous *Graceland* album, which fused African rhythms and vocal harmonies with American popular music. In a later album, *Rhythm of the Saints* (released in 1990), Simon combined the musical styles of South America with those of Africa and North America, to great effect.

At the same time, musicians from the non-Western world began to find success in the West. African dance music became fashionable in Europe, especially in France, and Youssou N'Dour (a singer from the former French colony of Senegal) became a major figure in Western pop music. In the USA, groups with a Mexican background, such as Los Lobos, gained a new popularity.

Stars of the Eighties

Like every decade, the 1980s produced a host of new and rising stars. Among the brightest were Michael Jackson and Madonna, along with Bruce Springsteen, Sting, George Michael and Prince. The top groups included Dire Straits and U2.

▽ *Prince's 1982 album, '1999', was followed by two, 'Purple Rain' and 'Parade', made with his band The Revolution, and in 1987 by a solo album, 'Sign O' The Times'.*

Madonna believed in keeping control:

'It's a great feeling to be powerful. I've been striving for it all my life. I think that's just the quest of every human being: power.'

△ *Lionel Ritchie fronts the line-up of rock stars taking part in the Live Aid concert in Philadelphia in July 1985.*

Michael Jackson confirmed his international status with the release of his *Thriller* album in 1982. Two years after its release, *Thriller* had produced seven Top Ten singles in the USA, and after selling 30 million copies worldwide it became the best selling LP of all time. Jackson was famous for his long and elaborate videos, which normally featured one of his brilliant dance routines. He lived in a vast mansion, with exotic animals, and seemed to prefer the company of children to adults. His colourful clothes and eccentric way of living continued to fascinate a global audience well into the 1990s.

Live Aid

The musical event of the decade was the holding of two charity concerts, called Live Aid, in July 1985. One concert was held in London at the same time as the other was held in the US city of Philadelphia, and both were televised live.

The inspiration for these charity concerts was the terrible 1984 famine in Ethiopia. Irish rock musician Bob Geldof (singer with the New Wave group the Boomtown Rats) was so moved by the plight of the starving people in Africa that he first persuaded a group of fellow musicians to produce a single called 'Do they know it's Christmas?' Sales of this record raised millions for famine relief at the end of 1984.

The heartfelt lyrics of 'Do they know it's Christmas?' included this chorus:

'Feed the World. Let them know it's Christmas.'

▷ *Mark Knopfler (right) and John Ilsley of Dire Straits, one of the top groups of the 1980s.*

This was followed by an American single – 'We are the World', written by Michael Jackson and Lionel Ritchie – and the Live Aid concerts. Thanks to a bigger satellite link-up than had ever been used before, the concerts were seen on television by an amazing 1.8 thousand million people around the globe. About $50 million was raised for famine relief, by record and concert sales and from donations sent in by the public. In helping the starving poor in Africa, the Live Aid concerts showed that the rich (and sometimes spoiled) pop music world really did think about other people. The concerts also acted as a showcase for top pop music acts, giving them worldwide coverage.

△ *Former Beatle John Lennon lived in New York with his wife Yoko Ono. This photograph of him (left) signing an autograph became famous because the fan in the picture, Mark Chapman, shot Lennon dead in December 1980.*

...Newsflash...

Brooklyn, New York, July 1983. Radical artist Laurie Anderson is in town to perform her six-hour work called *United States, Parts I-IV*. The piece contains a mix of music, words, cartoons and film clips. Anderson achieved stardom recently with her hit single 'O Superman'. She combines art, music and drama to make a special event for her audience. Anderson is one of several 'performance artists' who tries to use pop music to make us think differently about the world around us.

Innovations

Pop musicians in the 1980s were helped by the introduction of the 24-hour satellite music channel called MTV (Music Television). Now top rock and pop acts could have their music videos broadcast around the world, from Brazil to Japan. In the world of pop it was increasingly important to gain a worldwide audience; being big in just your own country was not enough. The growth of MTV made the production of videos vitally important. More than ever, groups and singers needed to have a strong visual appeal.

Compact discs (CDs) were another innovation that came to the aid of many musicians. CDs improved the sound for the listener. Also, since many music enthusiasts bought CDs to replace the ordinary (vinyl) records they had bought in the 1960s and 1970s, old

▷ Break dancing became a craze of the 1980s, with the dancers spinning on their heads, backs and hands, in an amazingly acrobatic way.

rock acts from the last 20 years or so did very well, as their recordings were sold for the second time.

With personal cassette players, invented in 1979, people could listen to music on their own while they were on the move. Over the decade, the Sony Walkman changed the way people listened to music.

Music talk

The most significant musical style to emerge in the 1980s was hip-hop, which was a development from Afro-American rap music.

66 99

A famous line from the rap song 'The Message' by Grand-Master Flash describes the terrible feelings caused by poverty and drug addiction:

'Don't push me, 'cos I'm, close, to, the, edge.'

The 1982 single 'The Message', by Grand-Master Flash and the Furious Five, was a highly influential rap record, which explained the problems of poverty, violence, racism and drugs that blighted people's lives in the USA's inner cities.

By the mid-1980s, hip-hop had extended the boundaries of rap (meaning 'to talk') to include not only music, but dance, fashion and slang. A hip-hop look developed among young Afro-Americans. It featured baggy jeans, baseball

Profile — Andrew Lloyd Webber (1948 –)

The main person behind the revival of musicals in the 1980s was the classically trained musician Andrew Lloyd Webber. Working with lyricist Tim Rice, he first found fame with the 'pop oratorio' *Joseph and the Amazing Technicolour Dreamcoat* (1968) and the 'rock opera' *Jesus Christ Superstar* (1971). Other successes followed in the 1970s, but in 1982 Lloyd Webber made theatre history by having three shows running simultaneously in New York and London: *Evita*, *Cats* and *Starlight Express*. He was knighted in 1992.

caps worn back to front, gold jewellery, and trainers – worn unlaced. The look quickly spread around the Western world among many teenagers. The 1984 album by Run-DMC – called *Run-DMC* – was a huge success. Hip-hop music moved out of the inner-city ghettos of the USA to become hugely popular worldwide.

The musical

In complete contrast to the tough world of hip-hop was the continuing success of the musical. One major hit was *Les Misérables*, which was based on a French novel about crime and punishment in 19th-century Paris. More important still was a series of musicals written by Andrew Lloyd Webber, which included

Cats (1981), *Starlight Express* (1983) and *The Phantom of the Opera* (1986). Although many music critics sneered at Lloyd Webber, his tunes proved immensely popular in Europe and the USA and his shows were regular sell-outs.

▽ *A duet from 'The Phantom of the Opera'.*

A LOOK AT
ART and ARCHITECTURE
IN THE '80s

The art world benefited from the 1980s financial boom. There was a lot of spare money about, which rich people used to buy works of art. This was especially true in the USA. New York's SoHo district was the centre of the enthusiasm for modern art.

Among the many US artists who established international reputations in the 1980s was Julian Schnabel. One of his trademark styles was to stick pieces of broken crockery onto his paintings. Another successful artist was Jeff Koons, who produced life-size statues of the singer Michael Jackson and a giant 'inflatable' bunny rabbit made from stainless steel.

▽ Jeff Koons's stainless steel rabbit, 1986, is over one metre high.

Even more extreme was Jenny Holzer, whose artworks consisted of messages written on T-shirts, postcards and electronic message boards. One such message, displayed in New York's Times Square, read simply: 'Money Creates Taste'.

Art in the subway

An artistic development which also came mainly from New York was graffiti art. Its origins went back to the elaborately drawn words and slogans that were sprayed on to New York subway trains as an act of vandalism. Bright colours and big letters were an essential part of this graffiti. In time, graffiti artists moved from the subway and began to cover any large surfaces in the inner city. There the painting caught the imagination of other artists and gallery owners. Soon, graffiti artists, like Jean-Michel Basquiat, were exhibiting their work in fashionable galleries.

Another artist who began in graffiti was Keith Haring, who used chalk to create distinctive squiggly line drawings on subway station walls. During the 1980s his work became immensely popular, and in 1986 he opened his own store in SoHo. Although his artworks could cost many thousands of dollars, he used his store – called Haring's Pop Shop

– to sell cheap items, such as decorated T-shirts and badges, for as little as $10. An active campaigner for AIDS charities, Haring died of the disease in 1990.

◁ *Self-portrait of a graffiti artist.*

Strange materials

Conceptual art was popular in the 1980s and involved artists spending time and thought in imagining the 'idea' behind the work of art. Leading conceptual artists included Joseph Beuys, a German, who brought many strange materials together. A famous series of exhibits he produced used just lard and felt.

Christo was a Bulgarian-born artist who moved to the USA and specialized in huge works of conceptual art. In 1983 he produced a work called *Surrounded Islands*, near Miami in Florida. It involved encircling eleven small islands with enormous pink plastic aprons. Later in the decade, Christo supervised the 'wrapping' of the Pont Neuf bridge in Paris (1985).

Keith Haring said that painting should be done quickly and without worrying over every little detail. He wrote:

'Graffiti art is an instant gesture. And because I'm capturing that instant, I do not believe in mistakes.'

...Newsflash...

New York, 11 November 1987. Vincent van Gogh's painting *Irises* was bought today by Australian tycoon Alan Bond for $53.9 million. Prices for major works of art have been rising steeply throughout the decade. The works are thought to be a good investment in times of economic turmoil. Van Gogh painted *Irises* in an asylum in 1889, and was unable to sell the picture in his own lifetime. The last time this painting came up for sale was in 1947, when it raised $100,000.

To many people Christo seemed very odd, but he claimed that he was trying to make people see objects in a fresh way.

▽ *It took Christo nine years to negotiate permission to wrap the Pont Neuf and to plan all the work involved.*

Profile

Richard Rogers (1933 –)

Born of Anglo-Italian parents, Rogers studied architecture in Italy. He believed that modern architecture must not be afraid to make use of the latest technology. After working with Renzo Piano on the Pompidou Centre in Paris, he was responsible for designing the Lloyd's Headquarters building in London, which opened in 1986. In both buildings, service lifts and air-conditioning ducts were not hidden; instead they were made a feature of the design, using bright colours and transparent materials. As well as designing buildings, Rogers lectured in architecture.

New buildings

The architectural world enjoyed a golden period during the 1980s, helped by the financial boom of the first half of the decade. Not surprisingly, some of the major buildings were built for financial institutions. Two of the most famous were the Lloyd's Headquarters in London, designed by Richard Rogers, and Norman Foster's Hong Kong and Shanghai Bank in Hong Kong.

A major building programme was launched in Paris by the French president, François Mitterand.

▽ *The Hong Kong and Shanghai Bank, opened 1986.*

A famous comment of Prince Charles on the modern design for the extension to London's National Gallery was that it was like:

'a monstrous carbuncle on the face of a much-loved and elegant friend.'

◁ La Grande Arche, Paris.

Most of the great modern buildings of the 1980s were very brash and modern and some people did not like them, saying that they did not fit in with other buildings around them. As a result, some architects worked in more traditional styles and designed buildings which looked back to the past. They deliberately used old materials such as brick and stone instead of new ones like concrete and glass.

" "

The director of the Louvre pyramid project, Emile Biasini, answered the many critics of the design:

'In ten years ... the arguments will have been forgotten. The ... French will regard it as another one of their classics.'

One of the most controversial works was designed by the US architect I. M. Pei: a pyramid which took centre-stage in front of the great French art gallery of the Louvre. Much of the main building work in Paris was concentrated around the area known as La Défence, including the great European landmark building La Grande Arche, designed by Danish architect Johan von Spreckelsen.

A masterpiece of the decade was the Neue Staatsgalerie in Stuttgart, Germany, whose architects were James Stirling and Michael Wilford. It combined different architectural styles in one exciting structure. Other key works were Jørn Utzon's National Assembly Building in Kuwait and Frank Gehry's California Aerospace Museum in Los Angeles, USA.

▽ The California Aerospace Museum.

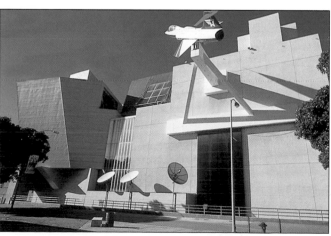

A LOOK AT
SPORT
IN THE '80s

Money and politics dominated sport – perhaps more so in the 1980s than in other decades. Television companies were keen to broadcast major sports. This would increase their numbers of viewers, and so enable the companies to make more money from advertising. The organizations running the sports that people liked to watch on TV – such as football – were able to demand high payments from the TV companies.

Politics and sport

Following the Soviet invasion of Afghanistan in 1979, the USA decided not to attend the 1980 Olympic Games which were held in Moscow.

▷ *Florence Griffith Joyner (known as 'Flo Jo') wins the 100 metres final at the Seoul Olympics, 1988.*

...Newsflash...

Seoul, South Korea, 2 October 1988. As the 1988 Olympics end, a new controversy echoes around the world. The Canadian sprinter Ben Johnson had set a new 100 metres record, with a time of just 9.79 seconds. But a subsequent drug test has revealed that Johnson had taken the banned substance anabolic steroids, which gave him an unfair advantage. Johnson has been stripped of his gold medal (which will go instead to second-placed Carl Lewis of the USA) and has been banned from international competitions for two years.

Many other Western countries joined the boycott and so these Olympics were not a true competition between the best athletes in the world. Much the same thing happened at the 1984 Games in Los Angeles, USA. This time, the Soviet Union and communist countries from Eastern Europe refused to attend.

Proper competition was restored at the 1988 Olympic Games, held in the South Korean capital of Seoul. The fact that top athletes both from the West and from communist countries had not competed for over 10 years gave these games a special interest. The women track athletes from the USA did particularly well, with the flamboyant Florence Griffith Joyner gaining gold and a world record in the 100 metres. Overall, however, the Soviet Union did best, with a total of 132 gold, silver and bronze medals. But the games was overshadowed by the Ben Johnson scandal, which revealed the high levels of drug use among top sports stars.

McEnroe often lost his temper with umpires. In 1981 he shouted one of his best-known remarks to an umpire:

'Man, you can not be serious!'

Tennis

In tennis, the men's game saw some epic battles between US stars John McEnroe and Jimmy Connors. Joining them at the top were the Czech-American Ivan Lendl, Swedish player Matts Wilander, and, in the second half of the decade, the young stars Boris Becker from Germany and Stefan Edberg from Sweden.

The women's game was dominated by Martina Navratilova. Although the American Chris Evert also fought hard, it was not until 1988, with the emergence of German player Steffi Graf, that Navratilova faced any serious challenge.

Boxing highlights

One of boxing's highlights in the 1980s was the competition between the great middleweights Sugar Ray Leonard and Marvin Hagler. Leonard defeated Hagler in 1987 to win the World Middleweight Championship. Heavyweight boxing was set on fire when the tough street fighter Mike Tyson defeated Michael Spinks to win the World Championship in 1988.

△ 7 April 1987: middleweight Sugar Ray Leonard (right) throws a punch at Marvin Hagler.

Profile

Martina Navratilova (1956 -)

Martina Navratilova dominated women's tennis in the 1980s, and also raised the women's game to new levels of power and speed. Born in Czechoslovakia, she later moved to the USA and became an American citizen in 1981. Navratilova won Wimbledon a record nine times, and by 1992, when she retired, she had won 54 Grand Slam events within a total of 158 championships – far more than any male or female player in the history of the game.

▷ *A Williams Honda driven by Nelson Piquet, world champion in 1981, 1983 and 1987.*

Motor and cycle racing

In Formula One motor racing, the top team was McLaren, which, with Porsche and then Honda engines, won five world championships. The runner-up team was Williams, with three world championships. The best drivers were the Brazilian Nelson Piquet and the Frenchman Alain Prost, with three world championships each, although one of the rising stars of the decade was the young Brazilian Ayrton Senna.

Cycling became an increasingly professional sport, with major teams from Europe and the USA competing for the major honours. The Tour de France remained the major test of a cyclist's strength, skill and courage. The course was 5,000 kilometres (3,000 miles) long, much of it over high mountains. One of the more surprising developments was the breakthrough of the US cyclist Greg LeMond.

He won the Tour in 1986, 1989 and then again in 1990, making him one of cycling's greatest stars.

Basketball and football

Basketball, a dominant sport in the USA, became increasingly popular in Europe. Basketball leagues with professional players became established in many European

Profile

'Magic' Johnson (1959 –)

Earvin 'Magic' Johnson became a major basketball star, playing for the Los Angeles' Lakers team. He earned his nickname for the brilliance of his playing style, which seemed almost magical! During the 1980s he became the most valuable player in the game.

In 1991, however, he retired from basketball after he found out that he was HIV positive (a series of symptoms which could develop into AIDS). He then went on to campaign about the dangers of HIV and AIDS, and to encourage young people to take up sports.

Profile

Michael Laudrup (1964 –)

This highly talented Danish footballer (on the right of the picture) began his career with the local team Brondbyernes. Then he was signed up by the giant Italian club Juventus, where he was involved in winning the World Club Cup in 1985. He later moved to Spain and played first for Barcelona – winning the 1989 European Cup Winners' Cup – and then for Real Madrid. Laudrup was typical of many young players of the time, who moved around Europe playing for the best clubs that could afford them. In 1986 he played for Denmark in the World Cup.

countries. Much of the new international interest in basketball was a result of the attention attracted by top players such as Michael Jordan and 'Magic' Johnson. These stars earned vast amounts of money by endorsing sportswear products.

But the most popular game in the world was still football, played by millions of people and watched by billions! The 1982 World Cup held in Spain was won by Italy. The next World Cup (Mexico, 1986) was won by an Argentinian team, led by the brilliant but unstable Diego Maradona. During a match against England, Maradona knocked the ball into the net using his hand. Although this was deliberate cheating – he

▷ *Argentinian football captain Diego Maradona shows off the World Cup trophy at the end of the final against Germany, 1986.*

cheekily called it the 'hand of God' – there could be no doubt that Maradona was the best footballer in the world at that time.

Football in England – the country which invented the modern game – went through a bad period in the 1980s. Crowd trouble was a particular problem, with gangs of so-called supporters from one club attacking the supporters from another. In 1985, British hooligans were responsible for the deaths of 39 supporters at a European game at Heysel in Belgium. In 1989, an even worse event took place at the Hillsborough stadium in Sheffield in England, when 95 people were crushed to death because of overcrowding and poor policing. As a result of these incidents, football stadiums and the organization of supporters were improved.

A LOOK AT
LEISURE and ENTERTAINMENT
IN THE '80s

The leisure and entertainment industries became bigger and more powerful during the 1980s. People throughout the Western world spent billions of dollars for their own pleasure and amusement.

Television

The biggest single form of entertainment was television, and during the 1980s it was transformed by new channels and by new ways of broadcasting. The CNN news channel was started in 1980, broadcasting only news, via satellite or cable. Few people at the time thought that CNN would succeed, but by the end of the decade its news stories were being transmitted throughout the world.

Another key global success story was MTV (Music Television), which was set up in 1981. MTV was designed not just for viewers in the USA but for an international audience interested in pop music. Although it only transmitted music videos, it had a great influence on pop music itself, helping launch the careers of singers such as Michael Jackson and Madonna.

The new TV channels did not rely on the old

◁ Aaron Spelling's TV series 'Dynasty' was the story of business tycoon Blake Carrington (John Forsythe), his wife Krystle (Linda Evans) and – the power-dressed villain – his ex-wife Alexis Colby (Joan Collins).

national and 'terrestrial' broadcasting systems, but used either satellite or cable. This was the beginning of a broadcasting revolution which would continue well into the 1990s.

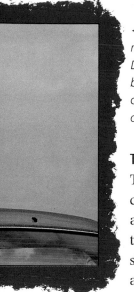

◁ *A new way of making home movies arrived with the camcorder. During the decade, TV programmes began to be made from humorous clips sent in by viewers from their own home videos.*

TV shows of the decade

The TV programmes that captured an international audience came mainly from the USA. *Dallas* was a drama show that was based around a wealthy Texas oil-family. The main character was the ruthless J.R. Ewing. When he was mysteriously shot and wounded, during an episode in 1980, television ratings around the world broke new records. At its peak, *Dallas* was broadcast in 91 countries.

'Dallas' was about wealth, greed and weakness. Producer Philip Capice said:

'Viewers love to see rich people more screwed up than they are. It makes them feel superior.'

US TV comedy also proved popular, including shows such as *Cheers* – about a bar in Boston – and *Roseanne*, the story of a blue-collar family in Middle America.

One other type of programme which became important was the confessional chat-show, where a presenter encouraged people to talk about problems in their lives. Chat-show host Oprah Winfrey became famous for the way she identified with the people on her show.

Profile

Oprah Winfrey (1954 -)

Oprah Winfrey entered television in the 1980s with a local chat-show based in Chicago. It was successful because she made her guests feel at home, especially as they talked about difficult problems such as homelessness and sexual abuse. Oprah was also prepared to talk about her own difficulties, including problems with her weight and with close relationships. In 1986 her show was broadcast nationally and became a ratings winner all over the USA. Oprah has been in several Hollywood films and was Oscar-nominated for her role in *The Colour Purple*.

Film director Steven Spielberg said that his early life was influenced by:

'growing up with three parents – a mother, a father and a TV set.'

◁ *In Steven Spielberg's 1982 movie 'ET, The Extra-Terrestrial', ET becomes friends with a young American boy, Elliott.*

films, such as the *Die Hard* series starring Bruce Willis. Less violent but equally popular was *Back to the Future*, starring Michael J. Fox as someone who goes back and forwards in time.

The development of computer animation enabled film-makers to produce ever-better special effects to amaze their audiences.

At the movies

Big Hollywood movies attracted huge audiences around the world. Steven Spielberg made some spectacularly successful films, such as *Raiders of the Lost Ark* and *ET*. Although he used many brilliant special effects, his real achievement lay in his ability to tell a simple story very well.

Ex-bodybuilder Arnold Schwarzenegger was the star of *The Terminator*, in which he played a cy-borg assassin from the future. The film was a big hit, and was followed by two sequels. The *Terminator* films also influenced other Hollywood

▽ *Science fiction and action films relied on the skills of special effects experts. In one film – 'Who Framed Roger Rabbit?' – the human actor even co-starred with a three-dimensional computer-animated rabbit!*

...Newsflash...

Milwaukee, USA, 21 August 1983.
A group of computer hackers, aged from 17 to 22, have broken into 20 of the country's major computer systems. Among the systems entered by the hackers was the top-secret nuclear research centre at the Los Alamos National Laboratory. Reports that other computer hackers have broken into different sites around the USA, including the Pentagon, have raised new fears about computer security.

As people bought video recorders (VCRs) to tape TV programmes, a new leisure industry started, of renting movies on video for people to watch at home.

▷ *Virtual Reality machines began to be installed in amusement arcades. Wearing the special helmet, users were able to interact with a three-dimensional world which seemed almost real.*

66 99

Computer expert Jaron Lanier was a pioneer of the computer-generated 3-D world he called Virtual Reality:

'It's the first place that exists between people like the physical world, except that it's totally under our control, unlike the physical world.'

Computers for play

The electronic revolution also changed people's leisure activities. Personal computers (PCs) had been intended for business use, but much of their popularity resulted from people using them to play computer games. These games became increasingly complex as the decade went on. The obsessional interest in computers shown by some young people became a concern in the 1980s. Parents tried to limit the time their children spent with their computers.

As well as games for PCs, the 1980s saw the development of console computer systems and games. Originally, these had been confined to large amusement arcade machines, but in the 1980s they moved into the home. The Pac-Man game of 1981 was a major advance in game technology, but the real breakthrough came with the Nintendo's Game Boy system in 1985.

The success of the CD as a means of storing information led to the development of the CD-ROM at the end of the decade. This was the beginning of the multimedia revolution, which would continue in the 1990s.

Getting fit

Although people were spending much time sitting down watching television or looking at computer screens, there was a growing movement towards taking part in sports and other healthy activities.

Rollerskating provided the origin for skateboarding, which developed into a major international craze in the 1980s. Another sport which made use of things from other activities was windsurfing, combining a surf board and a dinghy sail.

Mountain biking began in California, when young people started cycling down hilly trails. Soon, special bikes were being built with extra gears, stronger frames and wide tyres to cope with rough terrain.

△ Windsurfing was one of the great success stories among the new activity sports of the 1980s. Rather than just being a craze, it remained popular around the world.

Activities such as mountain biking and windsurfing became more than just sports, as people who took part in them wore special clothes and developed their own special languages.

Profile

Jane Fonda (1937 –)

US film star and political activist, campaigning for peace and a better environment, Jane Fonda attracted international attention in 1981 when she published *Jane Fonda's Workout Book*. The book, which encouraged women to improve their diets and exercise, was followed by music cassettes, a video – the top-seller of all time – and the setting up of exercise studios. Women worldwide followed Fonda's advice to get fit, and a new exercise industry was born. During the 1980s she continued to act. Films she appeared in include *On Golden Pond* and *The Morning After*.

Marathons and more

The new interest in healthy living reached an extreme with the development of mass marathons, which were held in major cities around the world. The idea behind mass marathons, which originated in New York, was to develop a race which would allow ordinary people to compete with recognized long-distance runners. The London Marathon, for example, attracted up to 20,000 runners, many of whom had never done much physical activity before. Many people were sponsored to run for charity, and some did it in fancy dress.

> ▷ April 1988: a 'sea' of marathon runners make their way towards Boston, Massachusetts, just after the start of the Boston Marathon in Hopkinton.

More restrained than running 26-mile marathons, but attracting even more people, was the growing interest in aerobics. Jane Fonda made aerobics popular throughout the world, especially among women. They found aerobics a useful and a social way of keeping in shape.

Shop till you drop

Shopping was nothing new, but during the 1980s it virtually became a new leisure activity. The development of big, enclosed shopping malls, complete with fast-food outlets, and vast out-of-town superstores changed the way in which people bought things. Going shopping became a 'day out' for many people.

Hello ...
Adventure holidays;
Indiana Jones;
Computer nerds;
Super Mario;
Sonic the Hedgehog;
McDonalds –
around the world

The world of leisure and entertainment grew ever more complex and expensive. The manufacturers of electrical goods – including personal computers, VCRs and the Sony Walkman – made fortunes because people were determined to enjoy themselves, no matter what the cost.

Date List

1980

18 April ▷ The former white-dominated African colony of Rhodesia is renamed Zimbabwe. A black majority government under Robert Mugabe comes to power after full democratic elections.

19 May ▷ Eight people are killed when the Mount St Helens volcano erupts in the USA. Dust thrown up by the volcano spreads around the world, affecting the global climate.

30 September ▷ Led by Saddam Hussein, Iraq invades Iran to capture the oil-rich province of Khuzistan. Eight years of bitter warfare begin.

4 November ▷ Former Hollywood actor Ronald Reagan is elected president of the USA.

8 December ▷ John Lennon, former co-leader of The Beatles, is shot dead by a fanatic outside Lennon's New York home.

1981

20 January ▷ 52 US hostages, held captive by the Iranians for 444 days, are finally released and will fly home to the USA.

29 July ▷ Prince Charles, heir to the British throne, marries Lady Diana Spencer.

6 October ▷ Egyptian leader President Anwar el-Sadat is assassinated by Islamic militants, angry at Sadat's peace treaty with Israel.

17 December ▷ Continuing strikes in Poland lead the government to introduce martial law.

1982

2 April ▷ Argentinian forces invade the Falkland Islands, and this leads to war with Britain. The British recapture the islands in June and force the Argentinians to surrender.

16 July ▷ The Reverend Sun Myung Moon marries 2,075 couples from his Unification Church at a mass wedding ceremony in New York.

18 September ▷ Right-wing Lebanese Christian forces murder Palestinian refugees in the Sabra and Chatila camps outside Beirut. The Israeli government is condemned for allowing the massacres to take place.

29 October ▷ In Spain's first democratic elections since the 1930s, a left-wing government is elected, with Felipe Gonzalez as leader.

1983

11 May ▷ A German journalist admits that he forged the recently published diaries of the German dictator Adolf Hitler.

24 June ▷ The space shuttle *Challenger* returns to base after a mission with astronaut Sally Ride, the first American woman to go into space.

23 October ▷ A Muslim terrorist drives a truck full of explosives into the US Embassy in Beirut, killing 216 people. Another explosion kills 58 in a compound used by French peacekeeping forces.

31 October ▷ US troops invade the small Caribbean island of Grenada and overthrow the Marxist government that had taken control.

1984

23 April ▷ French and US researchers independently announce the discovery of a new virus, which they think is the cause of AIDS.

31 October ▷ Indian Prime Minister Indira Gandhi is murdered by two of her bodyguards, Sikh extremists who accuse the government of discriminating against people of the Sikh religion.

10 December ▷ South African civil rights activist Bishop Desmond Tutu is awarded the Nobel Peace Prize. He believes in non-violent protest against the apartheid regime in South Africa.

1985

13 March ▷ After the funeral of Konstantin Chernenko, leadership of the Soviet Union passes to Mikhail Gorbachev.

1 September ▷ French and US researchers report finding the hulk of the *Titanic* in the mid-Atlantic, 73 years after the ship was sunk.

7 October ▷ Palestinian terrorists take over the passenger ship *Achille Lauro*, on a cruise in the Mediterranean. One American passenger is killed before the hostages are released.

21 November ▷ Ronald Reagan and Mikhail Gorbachev meet for the first time in Geneva. They discuss nuclear arms control.

1986

31 January ▷ Seven astronauts are killed when the space shuttle *Challenger* explodes shortly after take-off.

28 February ▷ Swedish prime minister Olaf Palme is killed by an unknown assassin while walking through the streets of Stockholm.

21 April ▷ US aircraft bomb targets in Libya. According to US officials this is 'punishment' for Libya's alleged encouragement of terrorism.

November ▷ Spilling of chemicals into the Rhine near its source in Switzerland is causing severe environmental damage throughout the river.

30 December ▷ President Reagan acknowledges that 'mistakes were made' in the illegal supply of money and arms to right-wing 'Contra' rebels in Nicaragua.

1987

30 May ▷ West German teenage pilot Matthias Rust lands a light aircraft in Moscow's Red Square. Russian air-defence officials are highly embarrassed by this publicity stunt.

20 October ▷ The world economy is shaken by the collapse of the US Wall Street Market.

10 December ▷ The USA and the Soviet Union sign an historic treaty to limit the size of their nuclear arsenals.

1988

16 May ▷ Some Soviet troops leave Afghanistan, the opening stage of a planned withdrawal. The Soviet Red Army fought the US-backed Afghan rebels for 8 years but was unable to defeat them.

19 September ▷ The Burmese Army takes over the country, ousting a new civilian government which had promised democratic freedoms.

8 November ▷ Republican candidate George Bush defeats his Democrat opponent Michael Dukakis to become the next president of the USA. Bush will succeed Ronald Reagan.

2 December ▷ Benazir Bhutto becomes prime minister of Pakistan: the first woman to head a modern Muslim state.

1989

24 February ▷ The Iranian government declares the writer Salman Rushdie's book *The Satanic Verses* to be blasphemous. They sentence him to death and issue a reward for his murder.

30 March ▷ The oil-tanker *Exxon Valdez* runs aground off Alaska, spilling millions of barrels of crude oil over the coastline. Millions of fish and seabirds are killed.

5 June ▷ Units of the Chinese army crush the Chinese democracy movement. Student demonstrators claim that as many as 2,000 people have been killed by the army.

10 November ▷ The Berlin Wall, which divided the city into two halves, is pulled down by demonstrators. This is a key event in the downfall of the East German communist state and a first step towards German reunification.

Glossary

apartheid

A political system in South Africa based on racial segregation, where a white government ruled over a black majority. The system ended in 1992.

blue collar

An expression used for working-class people – especially in the USA – because of the blue-collared overalls worn by many factory workers.

boycott

To refuse to take part or have anything to do with a person, organization or event.

cable TV

Similar to satellite TV in that many channels can be broadcast but, instead of using a satellite, the TV signal is transmitted to the customer's TV set using underground cables.

CD

Compact Disc: a small disc that can hold audio (sound) signals in a digital format – usually music – which can then be played back using a CD player. Generally superior to the older systems using (vinyl) records.

CD-ROM

Compact Disc Read Only Memory: similar in appearance to a CD, the CD-ROM is used in computers to provide large amounts of information, including text, sound and pictures.

CFC

ChloroFluoroCarbon, a chemical compound used in products such as aerosols and refrigerators. Found to be harmful to the environment, CFCs have been banned by most countries.

Cold War

A period of confrontation, from the late 1940s to the end of the '80s, between the Soviet Union (with its communist allies) and the USA and other Western states. Neither side wished to fight an all-out 'hot' war, so the conflict was limited to relatively minor 'cold' operations such as spying.

communism

A political and economic system where the government (or state) has total control of industry and agriculture. The Soviet Union was the first country to adopt communism, setting up a one-party system that prohibited all opposition.

conceptual art

A type of art in which the idea, or concept, is more important than the content of the work.

Contras

Right-wing guerrillas, supported by the USA, who fought against the left-wing government in Nicaragua.

corrupt

Using a position of power in a dishonest way, and open to bribery.

democratic

A democratic society is one in which all adults are able to vote at elections, and have a say in the way the government is run.

endorse

To show approval of a product, by allowing one's name to be used in advertisements for it. Celebrities are given money for endorsing products.

entrepreneurs

Business people who take the risk of investing money in the development of a new product or in the setting up of a company. They believe they will make more money eventually when the product or company succeeds.

ghetto

An area of a city in which poor people live, especially those from ethnic minorities.

graffiti

Words and pictures that are painted or sprayed on walls and buildings. Although usually illegal, much graffiti is of a very high standard, and some people consider it to be a special art form.

hackers

People who try to break into other computer systems. Usually very skilled in using computers, they often carry out hacking just for fun.

Hezbollah

An extreme Islamic fundamentalist organization whose name means 'Party of God'. It was supported by the Iranian government in the 1980s and used terrorist tactics against people in Israel and the West.

Hollywood

An area of Los Angeles in the USA which is the centre of the US film industry. Sometimes the word is used to describe a glitzy, spectacular event.

martial law

A system of law and order imposed over a country by its army, especially after unrest or during a breakdown in normal civilian law and order.

melt-down

The very dangerous condition describing the over-heating of a nuclear reactor, which causes radioactive material to escape into the atmosphere.

microprocessor

One of the smallest functioning units in a computer, and one of the most important. The number (and capability) of microprocessors in a computer determines the power of the computer.

militant

A person who feels very strongly about a cause – such as a religion or animal rights – and is prepared to take violent action in support of it.

pesticides

Chemicals used to protect crops by killing pests such as insects. Pesticides can also kill other forms of animal and plant life that are not harmful to crops. Many environmentalists think that pesticides are used too often and too heavily.

PLO

The Palestine Liberation Organization. Originally, the PLO was a group that used terrorism to try to destroy Israel, but during the 1980s it began to accept Israel as a proper state. Now, the PLO campaigns for the foundation of a Palestinian state alongside Israel.

pollution

The harmful action of man-made substances, such as chemical liquids and gases, on the environment. During the 1980s there was increasing international co-operation to try to limit the damage caused by pollution.

recession

A decline of activity and output in a country's economy, causing hardship and unemployment.

republican

In Ireland, this means a person who believes that Northern Ireland should leave the UK and become part of the Irish Republic. In the USA, a republican is a member of the Republican Party.

satellite TV

A new form of broadcasting which uses a satellite in space to transmit the television signal. Many more channels can be broadcast by satellite TV than by the traditional 'terrestrial' system.

socialist

A supporter of socialism, a belief that the government should play a central role in the way people live and that a nation's wealth should be shared equally among its people. Socialism is similar to communism, but not so extreme.

stock market

A market or system in which stocks and shares in major companies are traded to the general public using stockbrokers.

terrorism

The use of violence and intimidation to try to force a government to accept the demands of a particular group. Spectacular acts of violence are often employed to draw international attention to the terrorists' cause.

The people in the picture on page 4 are:
Front row, left to right:
President Reagan, USA; President Felix Boigny, Ivory Coast; Interim President Abdus Sattar, Bangladesh; President Chadli Benjedid, Algeria; Foreign Minister Hans Genscher, Germany; Prime Minister Pierre Trudeau, Canada; President Lopez Portillo, Mexico; Prince Fahd, Saudi Arabia; Foreign Minister Willibald Pahr, Austria; Foreign Minister Ramiro Guerriro, Brazil; Prime Minister Zhao Ziyang, China; President Ferdinand Marcos, Philippines.
Back row, left to right:
President Sergej Kraigher, Yugoslavia; President Julius Nyerere, Tanzania; Prime Minister Margaret Thatcher, Britain; Prime Minister Zenko Suzuki, Japan; President Forbes Burnham, Guyana; President François Mitterrand, France; Prime Minister Indira Gandhi, India; President Alhaji Shehu Shagari, Nigeria; Prime Minister Thorbiorn Falldin, Sweden; President Luis Herrera Campina, Venezuela; UN Secretary General Kurt Waldheim.

Resources

Books

Among the more accessible books on this decade are a couple of short volumes written for children and young people: *The 1980s* by Richard Tames (Franklin Watts, 1990) and *We Were There in The 1980s* by Rosemary Rees (Heinemann, 1993).

For older readers, the 1980s sections of *The Chronicle of the 20th Century* (JL Publishing, 1992) and *Our Times: The Illustrated History of the 20th Century* (Turner Publishing Inc., 1995) are very informative.

Relying heavily on news photographs is *The Illustrated History of the 20th Century*, with text by Rupert Matthews (Ted Smart, 1993).

Several novels published in the USA summed up the greediness of many people during the 1980s. They include Jay McInery's *Bright Lights, Big City*, Tama Yanovitz's *Slaves of New York* and Bret Easton Ellis's *Less Than Zero*.

The novelist and journalist Tom Wolf also looked at the decade with a critical eye in a book called *Bonfire of the Vanities*.

Films

In the USA, two notable films which gave a flavour of the decade were *Fatal Attraction* and *The Rain Man*.

The 1980s saw a renewed interest in the Vietnam War and several serious films were released which examined the USA's role in the war. These included Oliver Stone's *Platoon* and Stanley Kubrik's *Full Metal Jacket*.

In Britain, one of the more noteworthy films of the 1980s, which considered the problems of young people growing up into adulthood, was Stephen Frears' *My Beautiful Laundrette*.

Music

The theme of young people's dissatisfaction with the way the world worked was expressed in Pink Floyd's 1980 album *The Wall*.

On a more positive note, the biggest event of the decade was the combined UK/US Live Aid concert, which can be seen on video.

Two of the most globally influential artists of the decade were Michael Jackson and Madonna.

By comparison, the Irish group U2's album *The Joshua Tree* reflected a more serious side to popular music.

Art and architecture

Most art galleries in large towns and cities have paintings and sculpture from artists working in the 1980s. Leading artists working in this decade included Frank Auerbach, Francis Bacon, Joseph Beuys, Lucian Freud, Gilbert and George, Jenny Holzer, Jeff Koons and Julian Schnabel.

Quotations

The quotations in this book are from: Page 4: *The Observer*, 27 January 1980; Pages 8, 23, 31, 39: *Our Times: The Illustrated History of the 20th Century*, Turner Publishing Inc., Atlanta, 1995; Page 11: *Chronicle of the 20th Century*, JL International Publishing, 1992; Page 13: Bruce Sterling, ed., *Mirrorshades*, 1986, quoted in Robert Andrews, ed., *Cassell Dictionary of Contemporary Quotations*, Cassell, 1996; Page 14: Edmund Wright, ed., *The Bloomsbury Chronological Dictionary of Quotations*, Bloomsbury, 1993; Page 17: Amanda Heggs, quoted in *The Guardian*, 12 June 1989; Page 19: Valerie Steele, *Fifty Years of Fashion*, Yale University Press, 1993; Page 21: quoted in *The Guardian*, 23 October 1998; Page 29: Ronald Tamplin, ed., *Harrap's Illustrated History of the 20th Century: The Arts*, Harrap, 1991; Page 38: James Monaco, ed., *Virgin International Encyclopedia of Film*, Virgin, 1991.

Index